THE CANADIAN

Brass

BOOK OF EASY TRUMPET SOLOS

Edited by **Fred Mills** and **Ron Romm** of The Canadian Brass

■

All Selections Performed by **Fred Mills** and **Ron Romm** on trumpet,
and pianist Bill Casey

■

Plus Piano Accompaniments Only

CONTENTS
In a generally progressive order of difficulty.

* recorded by Fred Mills, trumpet
** recorded by Ron Romm, trumpet

The instrument pictured on the cover is a CB10 Trumpet from The Canadian Brass Collection,
a line of professional brass instruments marketed by The Canadian Brass.

Photo: Gordon Janowiak

To access audio visit:
www.halleonard.com/mylibrary
Enter Code
2043-5955-8022-5922

HAL•LEONARD®

7777 W. BLUEMOUND RD. P.O. BOX 13819 MILWAUKEE, WI 53213

www.canadianbrass.com
www.halleonard.com

Dear Fellow Brass Player:

We might be just a little biased, but we believe that playing a brass instrument is one of the most positive activities that anyone can pursue. Whether you're 8 years old or 60 years old, the ability to play a horn automatically creates opportunities of playing with other people in bands, orchestras, and ensembles throughout your life. But to keep yourself in shape and to better your playing, it's important to regularly work at solos. You might perform a contest solo for school, or play for a church service, or just for your family in the living room. Here's a book full of solos, in varied styles, that we think you'll enjoy learning.

All this music has been recorded for you by The Canadian Brass and is available to you online using the unique code found on page 1. Each song is provided twice: once as a full performance that includes the piano accompaniment and the solo instrument, and the other as the piano accompaniment only, which you can use in your practice, or if you wish, to perform with. The recordings of the solos that we have made should be used only as a guide in studying a piece. We certainly didn't go into these recording sessions with the idea of trying to create any kind of "definitive performances" of this music. There is no such thing as a definitive performance anyway. Each musician, being a unique individual, will naturally always come up with a slightly different rendition of a piece of music. We often find that students are timid about revealing their own ideas and personalities when going beyond the notes on the page in making music. After you've practiced for weeks on a piece of music, and have mastered all the technical requirements, you certainly have earned the right to play it in the way you think it sounds best! It may not be the way your friend would play it, or the way The Canadian Brass would play it. But you will have made the music your own, and that's what counts.

Good luck and Happy Brass Playing!
The Canadian Brass

FRED MILLS had an extensive performing career that preceded his joining The Canadian Brass. He grew up in Guelph, Ontario. After graduating from the Juilliard School of Music, he became principal trumpet under conductor Leopold Stokowski in both the American and Houston Symphonies. He also performed under Pablo Casals at the Casals Festival, and has played at the Marlboro Music Festival. For six years Fred was principal trumpet of the New York City Opera orchestra. Following this, he returned to Canada to take a position as principal trumpet of the then newly formed National Arts Centre Orchestra in Ottawa. In 1996, after 23 years with the ensemble, Fred chose to come off the road and lend his expertise to students at the University of Georgia.

RON ROMM was a child prodigy as a trumpet player, beginning his career as a soloist at the age of ten. By twelve, he was a member of his family's band; by age eighteen he was performing regularly with the Los Angeles Philharmonic. Ron attended the Juillard School, and while in New York established himself as a top freelance trumpeter in the city, performing with everything from the New York Philharmonic to the Radio City Music Hall Symphony Orchestra to Broadway shows (like Sondheim's *Company*) to the circus tours and ice shows. Ron joined The Canadian Brass in 1971, just when the group had been together about a year. Although he has little time for performing outside the extensive Canadian Brass concert schedule, he is sought after as a pre-eminent soloist in many musical styles.

BILL CASEY, pianist, grew up in Atlanta, and holds degrees in piano from Louisiana State University and the University of Missouri as Kansas City. He was assistant editor on the new G. Schirmer Opera Anthology, and has recorded several other albums for Hal Leonard. He resides in Kansas City, where he runs a music school for piano and voice students, as well as continuing to perform as both a pianist and singer.

SIMPLE GIFTS

Shaker Song
Arranged by Bill Boyd

WHEN JOHNNY COMES MARCHING HOME

Traditional American
Arranged by Bill Boyd

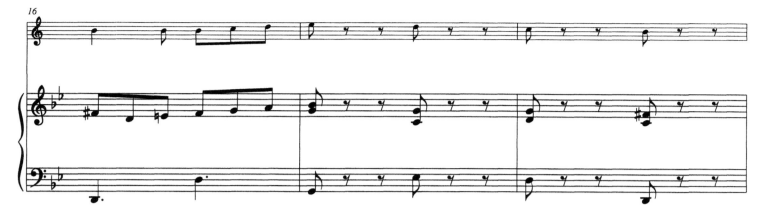

YANKEE DOODLE BOY

George M. Cohan
Arranged by Bill Boyd

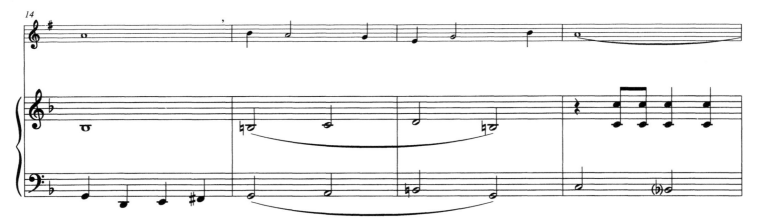

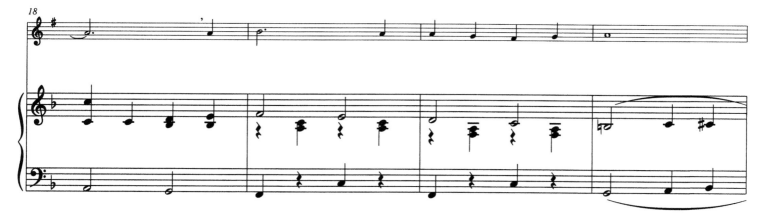

THE STAR SPANGLED BANNER

Words by Francis Scott Key
Traditional English melody
Arranged by Bill Boyd

LA CUCARACHA

Traditional Mexican
Arranged by Bill Boyd

Moderate rhumba

I AM THE MONARCH OF THE SEA
from H.M.S. PINAFORE

Words by W.S. Gilbert
Music by Arthur Sullivan

SIMPLE GIFTS

TRUMPET

Shaker Song
Arranged by Bill Boyd

WHEN JOHNNY COMES MARCHING HOME

TRUMPET

Traditional American
Arranged by Bill Boyd

Moderately (in 2)

YANKEE DOODLE BOY

TRUMPET

George M. Cohan
Arranged by Bill Boyd

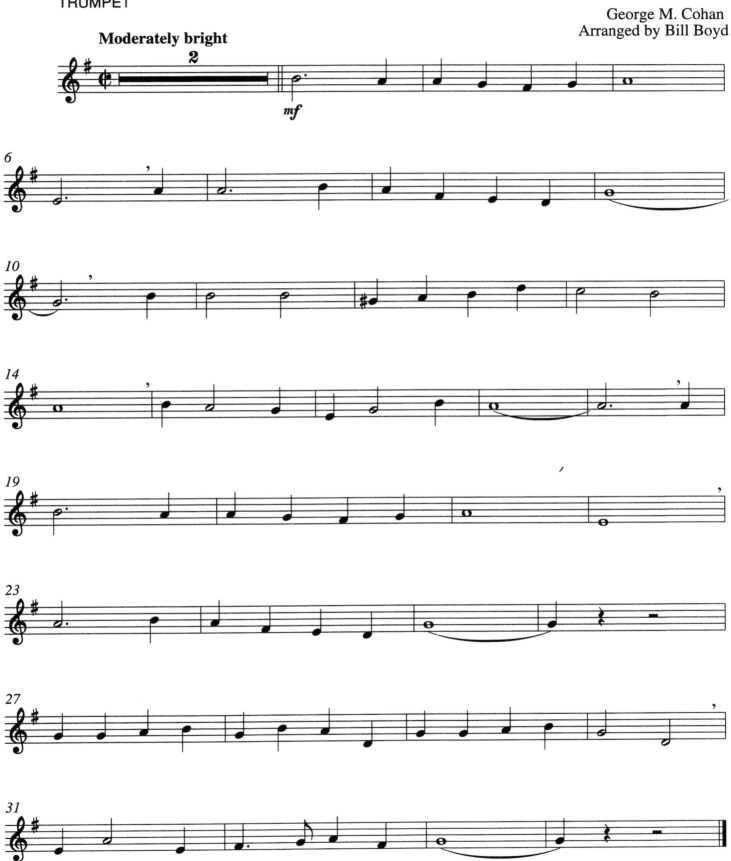

THE STAR SPANGLED BANNER

TRUMPET

Words by Francis Scott Key
Traditional English melody
Arranged by Bill Boyd

LA CUCARACHA

TRUMPET

Traditional Mexican
Arranged by Bill Boyd

I AM THE MONARCH OF THE SEA
from H.M.S. PINAFORE

TRUMPET

Words by W.S. Gilbert
Music by Arthur Sullivan

cresc.

f

mp

mf

f

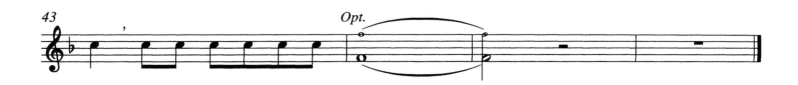

Opt.

f

FAIREST ISLE
(King Arthur's Address to Britain)
from KING ARTHUR

TRUMPET

Henry Purcell

ARIA
(Caldi sospiri)

TRUMPET

Raffaello Rontani

10

SHEEP MAY SAFELY GRAZE

TRUMPET

J. S. Bach

PASSEPIED

TRUMPET

George Frederic Handel

TO A WILD ROSE

TRUMPET

Edward MacDowell

With simple tenderness, not too slowly

THE MINSTREL BOY

Words by Thomas Moore
Welsh Melody known as "The Moreen"
Arranged by Bill Boyd

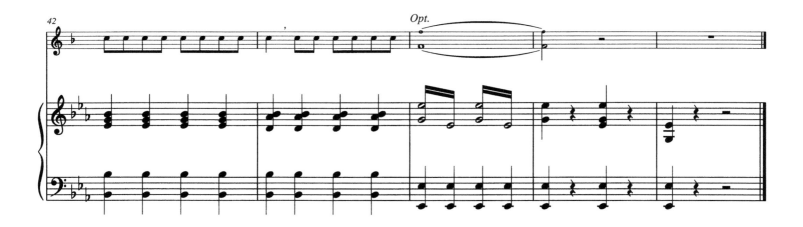

PASSEPIED

George Frederic Handel

FAIREST ISLE
(King Arthur's Address to Britain)
from KING ARTHUR

Henry Purcell

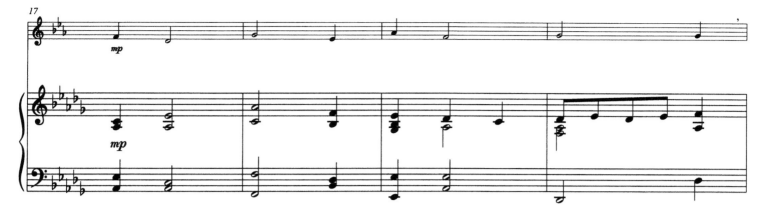

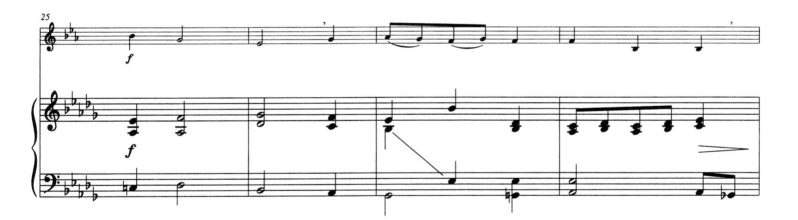

ARIA
(Caldi sospiri)

Raffaello Rontani

Assai espress., quasi arioso

Trumpet

Piano

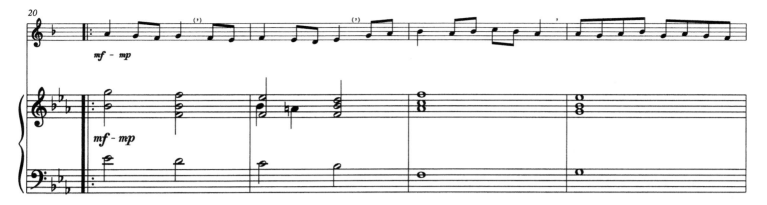

SHEEP MAY SAFELY GRAZE

J. S. Bach

TO A WILD ROSE

Edward MacDowell

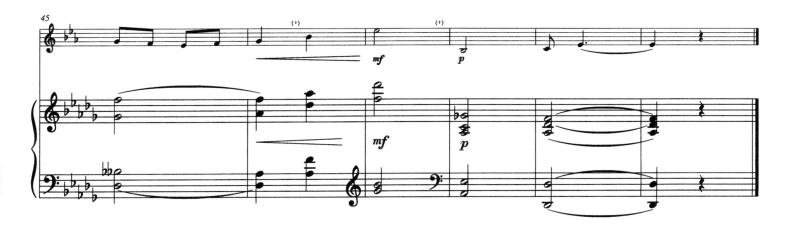

THE MINSTREL BOY

Words by Thomas Moore
Welsh Melody known as "The Moreen"
Arranged by Bill Boyd